That's How I Roll

(A hilarious, but fool proof, take on potty training)

D0681286

Rachel Poslick Jaques

Dedication

I would like to thank all of my family and friends for all their help and support. I need to give a very special thanks to my chief editor, or Mom as I like to call her. I couldn't have done it without you. One more big thanks to my husband for all his technical support. Without him this book would still be on notebook paper. And last but not least I need to thank my amazing children. This book is dedicated to you, for providing me with the inspiration and all the funny stories/pictures for this book. Oh and sorry for any future embarrassment this book may cause. Just remember Mom loves you!

Table of Contents

WARNING:

Please read the entire book before starting your potty training adventure

Are you thinking it might be time to potty train at your house?

Has your little one:

*Been bringing you diapers when they are wet?

*Going over to the corner to poop in their diaper?

*Started waking up with a dry diaper?

*Getting close to two years old or even older?

If you answered yes to at least two of these questions, then you are definitely ready to read this book. Don't worry I've made it into an easy list telling you exactly what to get and what not to get.

Rachel Jaques

CHAPTER 1

In the beginning...

"So there I was" with my first child thinking I was ready to potty train. When I walked down the baby/toddler aisle in Wal-Mart, I thought "Oh S#*t, I have no idea what I need". So I called my Mom, who loves to give advice, and she said that it was so long ago that those first few years were just a blur to her now. "Great, thanks anyway".

Next I went to the book store thinking I'd just read a quick book to get me started. No such luck, all I found was a bunch of thick 'text-booky' type books. Boring, who has time for that? I went back to Wal-Mart to wing it. This can be very overwhelming especially if it's your first child. How do you know what works and what doesn't? Fortunately that's where a 'potty-training whisperer' like me can be very handy. One of the best things about this book is that it saves you so much time and money.

So here's how it works: you get your child all excited to go to Wal-Mart or Target (if you're fancy). Tell them, 'today we're going to get big boy/girl underwear, no more diapers. Diapers are for babies, but I think you are ready to be a big boy/girl.' Really sell it to them. Remember they're two and they'll believe anything. Next, take them to the underwear aisle. Let them go crazy. Pick out three or four of their favorite packs of underwear. Make sure they think the undies are awesome- whatever they are passionate about, whether it's superheroes, cars & trucks or princesses. Now, also get several packs of just plain, sad white or solid color undies. Some packs have both and that's fine. Just make sure you separate the prints and solids when you get home. I'll explain all the details later. **No pull-ups.** I repeat, no pull-ups.

Next on the list we need a 'cushy seat'; they are awesome. These fit right on top of your toilet. It just makes the toilet opening a little smaller so they don't fall in. These come in different cartoon designs, one more awesome thing for your child to pick out. And if you don't already have one, be sure to grab a small foot stool so they can reach the potty and wash their hands. (Wash hands in the sink- not the potty) Please feel free to walk right past the $30 singing potty chair. Gross, the whole point of potty training is to make your life easier. If you still have to clean out a junior porta potty, you didn't save yourself any time. Not to mention, I've been to a lot of restaurant bathrooms and never have I seen a potty chair. Kids like to use the real toilet especially if it has a cartoon seat on it. Remember, it's all in how you present it! "Those little chairs are for babies. I think you're ready to use the big potty!" Plus, kids love to flush.

Now that's it for the baby aisle. Move your cart on down to the candy aisle. That's right; you need "kid currency", instant gratification or a short term goal if you will. Toddlers do not give a crap about money, but they love candy. Try to pick something you can count kind of like money. M&M's, gummie bears, or skittles usually work best. You put the bag of candy in a glass container, such as an old mayo jar. Place it either on the bathroom counter or close to the bathroom where they can see it. Now for the last thing on your list, you need two bottles of wine. You heard me right. If you're not a drinker that's fine, grab two of your favorite desserts or whatever little guilty pleasure that rewards you. Very important, do not skip this step.

Potty Training Survival Kit:

For the toddlers:
1. Underwear cartoon and plain. *No pull-ups*.
2. Cushy seat. No potty chair.
3. Step stool.
4. Kid currency such as M&M's or Skittles.

For the parents:
 2 bottles of wine or boxes of chocolate...

For some the excitement is just too much.

CHAPTER 2
Pull-ups: Amazing or another one of Satan's little tricks?

I'm sure your heart rate picked up a little bit in chapter one when you read 'No Pull-ups', but let me explain why. I know we are all very busy and those damn commercials make it look so easy and mess free. I think we over use pull-ups. "Hi, my name is Rachel and I was also a pull-up abuser." Trust me after potty training both with and without pull-ups, it's no contest. Here's my theory: pull-ups are confusing. Look at it from your toddler's point of view. Okay, I know for the last two years you've been peeing in these diapers, but not anymore because I got you new pull-up diapers. We don't pee in these diapers! To a toddler a diaper is a diaper. Most importantly, it doesn't feel gross if you pee or poop in a pull-up. If you pee or poop in regular underwear it's gross. It freaks them out. It runs down their legs and they're all wet. They don't like it and that is our goal. They will want to pick it up quicker if they are uncomfortable.

Now having said all of that I do think there is a place for pull-ups. Pull-ups are like vampires; they should only come out at night. I think they work great for that child who just can't hold it all night, but only after you've tried underwear first. Real underwear really helps emphasize that "you're a big boy/girl now, wearing real underwear just like Mom and Dad." I remember when I was potty training my middle son. He was and still is obsessed with trains. So of course he picked all train underwear. I was explaining, "you're so big wearing real underwear just like Mom and Dad." (FYI, my brother is a railroad engineer.) My two year old looked at me and said "Does Uncle Clay wear train underwear when he drives the big train?" and without skipping a beat I replied, "Oh yeah he does!" He felt so grown up. You don't get that with pull-ups.

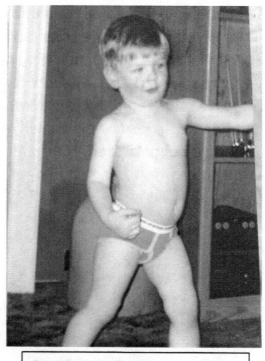

"CHOO-CHOO", oh yea rocking the train underwear.

CHAPTER 3
There's a new potty sheriff in town!

Oh yeah get excited! You, my friend, just got promoted to "Potty Sheriff". I know it sounds silly, but remember it's just you and your toddler and they think you're awesome! So this will help you remember to be firm and consistent. The most important thing for you to do is to be consistent. You would be surprised how far these three simple rules will go.

1) Have a good routine
2) Be consistent
3) Use a little common sense

These rules are not just for potty training. They will work for most of your parenting adventures. Remember, the morning you put those big boy/girl undies on, that's it-no going back. You have to stick to your guns! I'm telling you that first day is going to suck. There is no way around it, but don't give up. Stick with it and in about three to five days you'll be all done, diaper free. Don't worry if you've tried potty training before and failed; now you can start fresh with a plan in place and let them know you mean business. You're the law around these parts. Remember they're two and they'll believe

anything. Also you need to act like a salesman.
Really play up the big boy/girl thing and 'you're not
a baby anymore... so big... I'm so proud.' Get
excited and sell this whole potty training thing. The
more fun you make it the more they will want to do
it!

CHAPTER 4
2 Birds 1 Stone

Hope that's not a library book.

What could be better than having your little one potty trained? How about potty trained and off of the sippy cup in one week. As a parent we have enough to worry about, that's why my whole system is cheap and easy. I can admit that I am not the most organized parent. (Can you hear my family laughing?) I think that's why I am not really a "baby" person. Those first two years are so stressful for me. Just having that diaper bag packed all the time, to go visit Grams down the street, I felt like I had to pack half of the damn nursery. If you felt even a little of that, then you will love this. There's hope! I am having so much fun with my kids now. I am a much better parent now that we can just jump in the car and go. I don't worry about pull-ups, sippy cups, a change of clothes…. The less stress I have as a mom, the more fun I can have as a mom. The running joke with all my friends and family is that at Rachel's house once you're two, you're practically grown!

So here's the plan, since you are already getting your child excited about being 'big' and not being a baby anymore, just sneak this right in. "Sippy cups are for little kids, but you wear underwear now, you're big". The main reason I take the sippy cup away while I potty train is that I learned the hard way with my oldest. He must have had a fear of dehydration, because he would carry that sippy cup everywhere. When I started potty training him he had to go pee every 30 seconds and just a little bit. It drove me crazy and I was using pull-ups, so it was costing me money too. I was really starting to feel the pressure. You see, I was nearing the end of week four of a six week maternity leave with child number two. I knew that I had to have my two year old potty trained before I went back to work for two reasons: one, I've used all my vacation days for the next year, and two, with a new baby brother in the house we couldn't afford diapers times two.

That night while I was washing sippy cups and bottles in the sink it dawned on me, he has to pee every five minutes because he takes a sip and keeps playing, takes a sip, keeps playing, so his bladder was never full. Right then I decided no more sippy cup, no more pull-ups. The next evening I took the baby to Grams. Dad and I took our two year old out to a 'big boy' dinner and to Wal-Mart. We picked out all the underwear and several cups. I like the short wide cups because they don't spill as easy and that big kid cup wouldn't be complete without cartoons. Then we explained to him, no more pull-ups, no sippy cups because you're so big. Since we had a new baby in the house, he loved his big boy night out.

The new rules for the big cup are simple. I don't limit how much they drink; the only rule is the cup stays on the kitchen table. If your table is too tall, just set the cup somewhere in the kitchen where they can reach it. This way they drink a whole cup and then go play. By drinking the whole cup at once their bladder has a chance to fill up and it's easier for them to learn to hold it. I know what you're thinking, "mother trucker, I don't want to clean up all those messes by letting them have a real cup." Half the battle is picking the right cups. The cup should have a wide base so it doesn't tip over. It should be short so it's easier to handle and most importantly so if they spill, it isn't very much to clean. Make sure the cups are fun, like cartoons or their favorite color. Remember you're competing with the sippy cup, so this cup has to be awesome. Now what everyone needs for motivation: Start them out with milk or juice but if they spill, just water for a refill. I promise they will learn very quickly. Just think of how much easier your life could be next week. No more tearing the house apart to look for that last sippy cup only to find the one you weren't looking for in the toy box from a week ago, and it has that spoiled milk chunk in it. Or maybe that was just me. If it was just me, then it only happened one time. But seriously by age two they can handle a real cup. These days when we go places like car trips or go to the store, I let them use a small sports bottle with a squirt top. Still no mess and they're still a big kid. Plus, sports bottles are so much easier to wash they don't have that annoying rubber stopper to clean.

CHAPTER 5
D-Day or "Pee-Day"

WARNING: This may be one of the most frustrating and trying days in your parenting career so far. Now that we got that minor detail out of the way, lets potty train. Be Brave! You are now ready to potty train your little one. Make sure you have cleared three to five days in your schedule. If you work take off a Friday and a Monday, so you can really knock this thing out. All of my kids are two years apart, so I always potty trained on my maternity leave. The evening before you are going to start training is when you go to Wal-Mart and get your survivor kit. Take your little one with you; it will help get them excited about the process. If you've already tried potty training before and have some of these things on the list, just take them to dinner and start talking about how tomorrow we are going to potty train. Then swing by the store and let them pick out their "kid currency". I don't care if it's M&M's, skittles, marshmallows or stickers. Whatever they love, that's what you get. After you get home and get them all tucked in, go and set up the bathroom they are going to use. Make sure you have soap by the sink, your foot stool in the bathroom, "cushy seat" in place and your jar of "kid currency" on the bathroom counter. Also, separate the underwear in two piles; cartoons and solids. Now you are set up for D-day or day one.

As soon as your little one gets up, take them straight to the potty, and let them sit there for a few minutes and see if they can go. If they do, you have to get so excited! I mean the neighbors better think you just won the lottery! That excited. If they don't, it's no big deal. Either way when they get off the potty, they get to pick a pair of real underwear from the cartoon pile, and receive their "kid currency". My rule was always: one for just trying, two for pee, and three for poop. My friend who's a teacher used this system with her son and when she would give him the M&M's, she would have him practice counting and also identify the colors. Great idea Jill!

If there are any older siblings in the house, I would offer them one for helping. For an M&M my oldest would offer to take his little brother along with him whenever he needed to go. His theory was that he had to pee anyway, so he might as well get an M&M out of the deal.

Now remember I said to start them off in the cartoon underwear. Make sure you explain to them that whatever cartoon underwear you put them in doesn't like to be wet or dirty. "If the princesses get wet they will be so sad, and it will take me all day to clean them. If they get dirty I have to throw them away." And, make sure you really throw them away. I can't stress that part enough. This gives kids incentive not to have an accident. They will want to wear the cool cartoon underwear, and who wouldn't, especially if the other choice is plain solid white underwear.

I was discussing this method with a mom who told me that throwing away a child's favorite pair of underwear would be too traumatizing for a child. Keep in mind her child is almost four and not potty trained. I replied that throwing the underwear away is a consequence. Kids need to learn consequences to their actions. I personally think having the other kids make fun of you for crapping in your pants at four years old might be traumatizing. But that's just how I roll.

Now since you've cleared your schedule for three days and you're not planning on leaving the house, there's no need for getting them all dressed up. At least for the first two days I just let them run around in their underwear and maybe a t-shirt. If they're doing well on day three, I add clothes so they'll get used to pulling their pants up and down. (When you first add pants, elastic waists are the easiest.) This makes cleaning up the mess easier on you-the less laundry you have the better. I don't know about you, but laundry is my arch nemesis.

When they pee on themselves for the first time, they won't like it. It feels gross, and they are sad about losing their cartoon underwear. Once they have an accident I clean them up and explain you need to tell mommy when you have to potty. If the underwear is wet, I just throw it in the washer. I just put the lid of the washer up at the beginning of the day and any wet underwear, towels, or anything else that gets wet during the day gets thrown in. At the end of the day I just run one pee load of laundry and then everything is clean for day two. Now, if they poop in their new underwear, as I said earlier, I throw it away. For two reasons: One, it's gross, and I don't want to clean it. It's not worth me gagging and spending time scrubbing the dirty underwear just to save fifty cents. Two, most importantly when you throw them away make sure they see you. " Oh no, Lightning McQueen is ruined, and I can't fix that. We have to throw him away. I'm so sorry." This is crushing to your toddler, but that's good we're learning consequences. This is more motivation not to poop in their underwear. Once they've had an accident in the cartoons, now we go to the sad white underwear. Tell them to keep trying, and after nap we'll try another cartoon pair. After naptime start in the cartoons again, but if they have an accident, back to the whites. Each morning start in cartoons and see how long they can go.

Also remember that today we are using the big cup and only drinking in the kitchen. This will help fill their bladder up all at once and they won't have to go as often.

For Boys: to sit or to stand? That is the question. It is a common issue for moms who are usually in charge of potty training. I really think either will work, but I always taught the boys to sit at least for the first few days. Because I think sometimes they would get that feeling in their stomach to go and I'm not sure they know exactly which one was about to happen. So once they could tell me they had to pee, or mom I have to poop, then I would let them stand.

In fact this was a big issue with my daughter. She was so excited to go shopping and be big until I told her she had to sit down to pee. Because she has two older brothers, who apparently don't know that we have a door on the bathroom, she had always watched them pee. So when I made her sit down she screamed. My middle son who was four at the time tried to explain to her his take on the matter. "Girls have to sit to pee 'cause they don't gotta gun to shoot with." (Apparently my four year old felt the good lord had blessed him and the rest of the male population with their own personal super-soakers.) So if you're still wondering how I got my daughter to sit to pee, I had to physically hold her down just to get her on the potty. She's screaming, and then I asked if she would like an M&M? In mid-scream she paused and said "M&M's?" I gave her a whole handful and she never minded sitting on the potty after that.

OK, so other than potty training camp, it's just a normal stay at home and play day. The only difference is I don't let them sit on the furniture. It's much easier to clean the floor than it is the couch. Make sure every hour or so you ask if they want to try the potty? " Remember you get one M&M just for trying." Be prepared that you may have a bunch of accidents that first day. Mine averaged about six to eight on the first day. With my oldest he had eight accidents the first day. I was ready to scream, give it all up all together and send him to college in pull-ups.

This is where the first bottle of wine comes in handy. Instead of screaming and giving up all together, I suggest putting your little one to bed, and I will explain the night time plan in the next chapter. Turn on the T.V. or open a book, and relax with a glass of wine or some other treat while you finish up that load of pee laundry. Don't worry, day two gets better. That same child who had eight accidents on day one, came back and only had four on day two! So hang in there.

Chapter 6
Night Time

Night time is a totally different ball game. There are so many more factors. It's one thing to hold your pee for an hour while you're awake but to be able to do it for up to eight hours while asleep can be much more difficult. There can be a bunch of different reasons why a child pees the bed. So if your child is struggling with this, it's probably not his/her fault or even something he/she can control. Some children's bladders are just not big enough to hold it that long, others may have more complex medical problems, and other children just sleep so heavy they don't even know they've had an accident until morning. Most pediatricians say if kids don't out grow it by seven they start to look for a medical reason causing the problem. If you're having accidents at night be sure and let your physician know at their next check up, and you guys can make a plan from there. You did hear me say at their next appointment. Do not call the physician and make an appointment for next week because chances are they will outgrow it soon enough. The Doctor will probably just want to keep an eye on it especially if the child is still very young. Now having put that disclaimer out there, I do still have a plan.

For that first week I say put them in underwear at night and naptime, just to see if they can do it. If your child is in a toddler bed you don't have to worry about ruining the mattress most of them come with a plastic coating. If your child has already transitioned to a real mattress you may want to get a plastic sheet. If you use the plastic sheet you will still want to put a regular sheet over it. Alright, now that our mattress is protected we can move on. With my three I had very different experiences. One son I put in underwear and the first two nights went great. Then I woke up in the middle of night three to a blood curdling scream. I ran in to see if he was hurt or bleeding, nope he had just peed the bed. That child hated the feeling of being wet so bad that he never peed the bed again. Another one had accidents off and on until about three and a half and then I guess just outgrew it. I think that one didn't have a big enough bladder to make it all night. Then I have one child who I love very much, but who drives me crazy at the same time. When I go to wake this child up in the morning, I find the kid is soaked along with the bed and the sheets, and has no idea. This child is a very heavy sleeper, and up until about age five, wet the bed on a regular basis. At six the accidents were few. It seemed like the more exhausted the kids were when they went to bed the more likely that one was to have an accident. Days like the first week of school, sports tournaments, t-ball or soccer practices, or even swimming all day were likely culprits. Again it's just something they have to outgrow. I have heard that a lot of it is genetic. If one parent was a bed wetter, it's more likely that one of your kids will be.

Here are the tips I use to keep accidents to a minimum. If possible, I take them off fluids about two hours before bed. They may have one sip of water just before bed. Also make sure they get in the habit of peeing before bed; this rule applies for naps as well. Make sure you go potty right before nap. They are less likely to have an accident if you go to sleep on an empty bladder. Also make sure you have night lights in the child's room, in the hallway and especially in the bathroom. Even if they wake-up to go potty, they will still be sleepy. So make it easy for them to see where they need to go. Also try not to get angry or punish your child for night accidents. Nobody wants to pee the bed, and it truly may be something they physically can't do yet. So it's not fair to punish for that. In fact, it may make it worse. Another reason some kids wet the bed is stress. I know what you're thinking: kids don't have stress. Well if a kid is going to bed every night worried that if they pee the bed their parents will yell or spank them, that's stress. And, it will only make your problem worse. In addition, if there is something stressful in the child's life, such as divorce, or a death in the family, or whatever, this may be affecting their night time routine. You can't eliminate these stresses just be aware and compassionate. Good night, may your dreams be sweet and very dry!

Chapter 7
Light at the end of the tunnel

Alright, we've made it through day one, and we're on to days two, three, and four. This is where we separate the sheriffs from the deputies. A lot of people try hard for one day or even a day and a half to potty train with real underwear, and as you may soon find out it can be very frustrating. I don't think people prepare you for how frustrating that first day can be. Here's the good news, if you really stick to the same routine we laid out in day one, day two will be much easier. You will have half as many accidents as the day before. Even though some may say that's stressful, I say that's progress. Stick with it and days three and four you should only have one or two accidents, and by day five, halleluiah. Rome wasn't built in a day you know, but potty training can be done in three to five days. So many people struggle with potty training just because they're not consistent, and don't stick with it long enough. I know we all love instant gratification, we want it now. This is why I say you really need to clear your schedule for about three to five days. Take that day or two off work and really knock this thing out. For those of you who are reading this thinking, I'm too busy or I can't afford to take a day off to do this. I wrote this book for you. You can't afford not to do this.

Look around at your friends buying pull-ups for months going around with half trained children. Spending all that time and money, when in three days it can be done, handled. You roll up your sleeves and really dedicate some time to this.

Remember the old saying 'it takes a village'? Well it's time to get the village involved. I want you to tell your friends, family, daycare teachers, etc. all that you're going to be working on potty training. This can be helpful in several ways. One, it helps hold you accountable, because now whenever you talk to someone they'll say, "So, how's that potty training going?" You have to stick with it so you can say "Easy, in fact we're already done." The second reason is so that anyone who comes over to visit will ask your little one and they can do the bragging themselves. Your family and friends can tell them how great they're doing and also how proud they are. Grandparents are the best audience. I know all of my kids at age two, and even now, love to call their grandparents and brag. Hell I'm an adult and I still call my Nana to brag if something good happens. So, with each milestone, let them get on the phone and brag to someone. The first time they pee in the toilet, the first time they go accident free, drinking from the big cup, are now celebrations that need be reported. The more positive reinforcement they get, the more they will want to succeed.

For all you single moms trying to potty train boys, I have a funny story. I know a single mom who had to potty train her son all by herself. Well one day her brother, the little boy's uncle, went out to eat with them and took the little boy to the bathroom. The uncle came back a few minutes later with the boy just shaking his head. When the mom asked what happened, the uncle informed her that "when guys pee we don't dab the end with a square of toilet paper, we just shake it and go". (That could be traumatizing in the lockeroom!) This is another way I feel the village comes in very handy. As women we don't know all the proper 'urinal etiquette', so if you are a single mom potty training boys, make sure anytime they're with grandpa, uncle, or other male friends/family members, that they take the boys to the bathroom and show them how it's done. This also helps them feel like they are one of the big boys.

As with day one, the best way to make days two through five successful is to be consistent. You have to continue to ask your little one, do you have to go potty. Another part of being consistent is making sure everyone knows the rules and Dad needs to be on the same page with potty training. If the parents aren't together and child splits time at two houses or goes to grandma's for the weekend, they need to know your potty training rules so your little one doesn't regress or get confused.

Another question I often hear debated is whether or not to let boys pee outside? I always politely reply, "you bet your sweet ass I do!" That's win-win for me. I want my kids to play outside. Good exercise wears them out, and it helps keep my house clean. Here's part of the problem with potty training boys. A lot of them just don't care if they pee their pants. This is one reason some boys are harder to train. It's just not important enough to them to put the Tonka trucks down, get out of the sandbox and to go inside. So, they'll just pee their pants and keep right on playing. However if you allow them to pee outside, they think that's awesome. They never miss a chance to use their 'super-soakers'. They can pee on a tree, or a fence; oh the possibilities. Now to keep it classy I only let boys pee in the backyard. I'm sorry to report that it has been my experience that guys of all ages still love to pee outside. My boys are clearly not alone! I snapped this photo at a recent practice.

One more issue a lot of people run into while potty training is poop in the potty. For some reason the child will pick up peeing in the potty very quickly and then struggle with pooping in the potty. Now two of my test families weren't throwing away the underwear so make sure if they poop in their awesome cartoon underwear they go in the trash. It's not that the child isn't smart enough to understand, either they're just being stubborn, or they may even be scared of pooping in the toilet. So here's what worked really well for these kids. It didn't seem to matter what the underlying reason for not wanting to poop in the potty, the same tricks fixed them both. It turns out they just needed a little more motivation so we stepped up the ante a bit. If you're having this problem, I want you to take them back to Wal-Mart and let them pick out another awesome pack of underwear and you can go grab some sad whites if needed. Then take them down the toy aisle and let them pick out an awesome twenty or thirty dollar toy, whatever they're into. Let them touch it, hold it, really fall in love with it. Then I want you to get down on their level and place the toy back on the shelf and explain when you start pooping in the potty I'll bring you back and I'll buy you that awesome toy. Next swing by the sticker section and let them pick out some super cool stickers, whatever catches their eye. Now when you get home explain to your little one that we need to start pooping in the potty. Put the package of new cartoon underwear on their dresser (still in the package). Explain to them, that underwear is for big kids who poop in the potty. So when you start pooping in the potty, we'll open these. Next you and your little one are going to make a sticker board together. Take a blank piece of paper and write 1, 2, 3, 4, 5 on the paper. After the five draw or paste a picture from a catalogue of whatever toy your little one fell in love with at the store. (look online) Now, go post it at eye level in the bathroom. Explain that every time you poop in the potty we will put one of your awesome new stickers over the numbers. Once you've pooped in the potty five times we can go back to the store and get that toy you wanted. Now they have a lot more incentive to poop in the potty. They get three of their "kid currencies" and a sticker that gets them closer to their toy, and they get to open their new pack of underwear. This problem seems to be more common in boys who often are developmentally a little behind girls and may not be ready early.

My Mom tells the story of training my younger siblings, who are boy-girl twins. One day Becca was sitting on the potty doing what she was supposed to and Clay was sitting on the edge of the bathtub encouraging her. She finished and he clapped for her. Mom asked Clay if he wanted to try and he just grinned and said "nope" and walked out of the bathroom. A month or two later he decided he was ready and we are happy report that even though his wife doesn't think he's very well trained in many areas, he has mastered this one.

Chapter 8
Victory Sweet Victory

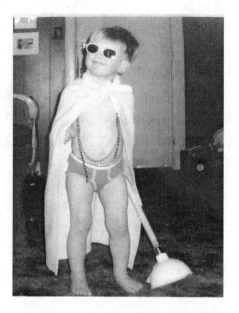

Break out the Queen music! "We are the champions". Crack open that last bottle of wine. We made it! Once your child has gone a few days in a row with no accidents during the day, that my friend is what we call potty trained. Now for the fun part, we need to alert the village and let them know about our success. Call Grandma and let your little one tell them the big news. They will be so excited. You need to discuss in advance with the grandparents to see if they would be interested in providing the 'trophy'. Every winner needs a trophy. I know toddlers aren't into real trophies yet but they like toys and fun. Don't worry, most grandparents will be happy to help with this part. They get a chance to spoil their grandkids and they'll feel like they got to help out. My mom was always very good about this. After she got the "I'm all potty trained" call she would go pick out a special toy she knew they would love or that they had asked for, and deliver it. She'd tell that child how proud she was and so excited for them. "Now that you're a big boy/girl and you worked so hard to learn to go potty, I bought you this special toy." If you had one of those children who already got a toy for pooping in the potty, then maybe Grandma or Grandpa takes them out for a big boy/girl day of fun. If your family lives out of town, maybe have them send a care package. I really think it builds their little self esteem when other people get excited and proud of them.

Now, don't get too cocky. Just because your child is potty trained doesn't mean that you won't ever have to remind them. This is especially true with boys who become sidetracked so easily. Remember they're young and still need lots of direction. Hell mine are eight, six and four and to this day before we leave the house I ask if anyone needs to go to the bathroom. Also don't be surprised if in the next few months you have an accident or two. These are usually timing issues like not being able to get pants unbuttoned or not being able to find a bathroom quick enough. I swear a toddler can go from not needing to pee at all, to jumping up and down doing the pee pee dance in a matter of minutes. Assure them that accidents are normal and to just make sure next time they use the potty. We don't want to regress.

Another common accident happens that first time they get diarrhea. Explain to them it's just because they're sick. Looking back on some of those stressful or embarrassing times are now some of my favorite memories. Here's a good example: my oldest was about three or so, and we were at my mom and step-dad's house. My son had been fully potty trained for at least a year so I didn't think anything about it when he went to the bathroom alone. Well, my step-dad (Gramps) went into the bathroom a little later and came to me just laughing. When I asked what was so funny, he said," your son is quite the artist. He's a real "*poop-caso*." Puzzled I ran into the bathroom and what was on the wall staring at me? Oh yeah you guessed it: a smiley face finger painted with poop. (Kids, they make you so proud.) So I have to drag my son in there and explain to him that it's not brown finger paint coming out of his bottom that it's poop and it's gross. "Keep it in the toilet, and if it gets on your hands, wash them." You would think some things would just be understood. When you find yourself getting too stressed or embarrassed, just think about what a hilarious story it will be some day!

Ok, you **are** now ready to start your own potty training adventure and we want to hear about it. So please go to our *facebook* page http://www.facebook.com/pages/Thats-How-I-Roll-A-hilarious-take-on-potty-training/326765594035617. We hope you will add your own posts, ask questions and even upload pictures of your potty training champ! Good luck and happy training!

About the Author:

Rachel, a native of Enid, OK, now lives in Moore, OK with her husband, Nick, and their three kids. She is a respiratory therapist at The Oklahoma Heart Hospital which she enjoys, but what she and her family love are sports. Between Rachel and her husband they help coach eleven youth teams in four different sports all named the Storm, and of course all three children play for these teams. Go Storm!! But no matter what the activity or sport, most of all she loves spending time with her family and friends.

CPSIA information can be obtained at www.ICGtesting.com
Printed in the USA
LVOW05s2329040314

376014LV00023B/1209/P

9 780615 605135